Table Of Co

Book Title	Author	Page

Book Title	Author	Page

Book Title	Author	Page

Book Title	Author	Page

Book Title	Author	Page

Book Title ______________________

Author ______________________ Nationality ______________________

Genre ______________________ Year ______________________ Pages ____________

Memorable Quote	Page Number

Characters

Plot Summary

Notes

Rating ☆ ☆ ☆ ☆ ☆

Book Title ______________________

Author ______________________ Nationality ______________________

Genre ______________________ Year ______________________ Pages ______________________

Memorable Quote	Page Number

Characters

Plot Summary

Notes

Rating ☆ ☆ ☆ ☆ ☆

Book Title ____________________

Author ____________________ Nationality ____________________

Genre ____________________ Year ____________________ Pages ____________

Memorable Quote	Page Number

Characters

Plot Summary

Notes

Rating ☆ ☆ ☆ ☆ ☆

Book Title ______________________

Author ______________________ Nationality ______________________

Genre ______________________ Year ______________________ Pages ______________________

Memorable Quote	Page Number

Characters

Plot Summary

Notes

Rating ☆ ☆ ☆ ☆ ☆

Book Title ____________________

Author ____________________ Nationality ____________________

Genre ____________________ Year ____________________ Pages ____________

Memorable Quote	Page Number

Characters

Plot Summary

Notes

Rating ☆ ☆ ☆ ☆ ☆

Book Title

Author

Nationality

Genre

Year

Pages

Memorable Quote	Page Number

Characters

Plot Summary

Notes

Rating ☆ ☆ ☆ ☆ ☆

Book Title ______________________

Author ______________________ Nationality ______________________

Genre ______________________ Year ______________________ Pages ______________________

Memorable Quote	Page Number

Characters

Plot Summary

Notes

Rating ☆ ☆ ☆ ☆ ☆

Book Title ______________________

Author ______________________ Nationality ______________________

Genre ______________________ Year ______________________ Pages ______________________

Memorable Quote	Page Number

Characters

Plot Summary

Notes

Rating ☆ ☆ ☆ ☆ ☆

Book Title ______________________

Author ______________________ Nationality ______________________

Genre ______________________ Year ______________________ Pages ____________

Memorable Quote	Page Number

Characters

Plot Summary

Notes

Rating ☆ ☆ ☆ ☆ ☆

Book Title ____________________

Author ____________________ Nationality ____________________

Genre ____________________ Year ____________________ Pages ____________

Memorable Quote	Page Number

Characters

Plot Summary

Notes

Rating ☆ ☆ ☆ ☆ ☆

Book Title ______________________

Author ______________________ Nationality ______________________

Genre ______________________ Year ______________________ Pages ____________

Memorable Quote	Page Number

Characters

Plot Summary

Notes

Rating ☆ ☆ ☆ ☆ ☆

Book Title

Author

Nationality

Genre

Year

Pages

Memorable Quote	Page Number

Characters

Plot Summary

Notes

Rating ☆ ☆ ☆ ☆ ☆

Book Title ____________________

Author ____________________ Nationality ____________________

Genre ____________________ Year ____________________ Pages ____________________

Memorable Quote	Page Number

Characters

Plot Summary

Notes

Rating ☆ ☆ ☆ ☆ ☆

Book Title ______________________

Author ______________________ Nationality ______________________

Genre ______________________ Year ______________________ Pages ______________________

Memorable Quote	Page Number

Characters

Plot Summary

Notes

Rating ☆ ☆ ☆ ☆ ☆

Book Title ____________________

Author ____________________ Nationality ____________________

Genre ____________________ Year ____________________ Pages ____________________

Memorable Quote	Page Number

Characters

Plot Summary

Notes

Rating ☆ ☆ ☆ ☆ ☆

Book Title ______________________

Author ______________ Nationality ______________

Genre ______________ Year ______________ Pages ________

Memorable Quote	Page Number

Characters

Plot Summary

Notes

Rating ☆ ☆ ☆ ☆ ☆

Book Title ______________________

Author ______________________ Nationality ______________________

Genre ______________________ Year ______________________ Pages ____________

Memorable Quote	Page Number

Characters

Plot Summary

Notes

Rating ☆ ☆ ☆ ☆ ☆

Book Title ______________________

Author ______________________ Nationality ______________________

Genre ______________________ Year ______________________ Pages ____________

Memorable Quote	Page Number

Characters

Plot Summary

Notes

Rating ☆ ☆ ☆ ☆ ☆

Book Title ______________________

Author ______________________ Nationality ______________________

Genre ______________________ Year ______________________ Pages ______________________

Memorable Quote	Page Number

Characters

Plot Summary

Notes

Rating ☆ ☆ ☆ ☆ ☆

Book Title

Author

Nationality

Genre

Year

Pages

Memorable Quote	Page Number

Characters

Plot Summary

Notes

Rating ☆ ☆ ☆ ☆ ☆

Book Title ____________________

Author ____________________ Nationality ____________________

Genre ____________________ Year ____________________ Pages __________

Memorable Quote	Page Number

Characters

Plot Summary

Notes

Rating ☆ ☆ ☆ ☆ ☆

Book Title ______________________

Author ______________________ Nationality ______________________

Genre ______________________ Year ______________________ Pages ______________________

Memorable Quote	Page Number

Characters

Plot Summary

Notes

Rating ☆ ☆ ☆ ☆ ☆

Book Title ______________________

Author ______________________ Nationality ______________________

Genre ______________________ Year ______________________ Pages ____________

Memorable Quote	Page Number

Characters

Plot Summary

Notes

Rating ☆ ☆ ☆ ☆ ☆

Book Title ____________________

Author ____________________ Nationality ____________________

Genre ____________________ Year ____________________ Pages ____________

Memorable Quote	Page Number

Characters

Plot Summary

Notes

Rating ☆ ☆ ☆ ☆ ☆

Book Title ______________________________

Author ____________________ Nationality ____________________

Genre ____________________ Year ____________________ Pages ____________

Memorable Quote	Page Number

Characters

Plot Summary

Notes

Rating ☆ ☆ ☆ ☆ ☆

Book Title ______________________

Author ______________________ Nationality ______________________

Genre ______________________ Year ______________________ Pages ______________

Memorable Quote	Page Number

Characters

Plot Summary

Notes

Rating ☆ ☆ ☆ ☆ ☆

Book Title ______________________________

Author ____________________ Nationality ____________________

Genre ____________________ Year ____________________ Pages __________

Memorable Quote	Page Number

Characters

Plot Summary

Notes

Rating ☆ ☆ ☆ ☆ ☆

Book Title ______________________

Author ______________ Nationality ______________

Genre ______________ Year ______________ Pages ______________

Memorable Quote	Page Number

Characters

Plot Summary

Notes

Rating ☆ ☆ ☆ ☆ ☆

Book Title ______________________________

Author ____________________ Nationality ____________________

Genre ____________________ Year ____________________ Pages ____________

Memorable Quote	Page Number

Characters

Plot Summary

Notes

Rating ☆ ☆ ☆ ☆ ☆

Book Title ______________________

Author ______________________ Nationality ______________________

Genre ______________________ Year ______________________ Pages ______________________

Memorable Quote	Page Number

Characters

Plot Summary

Notes

Rating ☆ ☆ ☆ ☆ ☆

Book Title ______________________________

Author ____________________ Nationality ____________________

Genre ____________________ Year ____________________ Pages __________

Memorable Quote	Page Number

Characters

Plot Summary

Notes

Rating ☆ ☆ ☆ ☆ ☆

Book Title ______________________

Author ______________ Nationality ______________

Genre ______________ Year ______________ Pages ______________

Memorable Quote	Page Number

Characters

Plot Summary

Notes

Rating ☆ ☆ ☆ ☆ ☆

Book Title ______________________

Author ______________________ Nationality ______________________

Genre ______________________ Year ______________________ Pages ____________

Memorable Quote	Page Number

Characters

Plot Summary

Notes

Rating ☆ ☆ ☆ ☆ ☆

Book Title ______________________

Author ______________________ Nationality ______________________

Genre ______________________ Year ______________________ Pages ____________

Memorable Quote	Page Number

Characters

Plot Summary

Notes

Rating ☆ ☆ ☆ ☆ ☆

Book Title ______________________

Author ______________________ Nationality ______________________

Genre ______________________ Year ______________________ Pages ______________

Memorable Quote	Page Number

Characters

Plot Summary

Notes

Rating ☆ ☆ ☆ ☆ ☆

Book Title ______________________

Author ______________________ Nationality ______________________

Genre ______________________ Year ______________________ Pages ______________

Memorable Quote	Page Number

Characters

Plot Summary

Notes

Rating ☆ ☆ ☆ ☆ ☆

Book Title ______________________

Author ______________________ Nationality ______________________

Genre ______________________ Year ______________________ Pages ____________

Memorable Quote	Page Number

Characters

Plot Summary

Notes

Rating ☆ ☆ ☆ ☆ ☆

Book Title ____________________

Author ____________________ Nationality ____________________

Genre ____________________ Year ____________________ Pages ____________

Memorable Quote	Page Number

Characters

Plot Summary

Notes

Rating ☆ ☆ ☆ ☆ ☆

Book Title ______________________

Author ______________________ Nationality ______________________

Genre ______________________ Year ______________________ Pages ______________________

Memorable Quote	Page Number

Characters

Plot Summary

Notes

Rating ☆ ☆ ☆ ☆ ☆

Book Title ____________________

Author ____________________ Nationality ____________________

Genre ____________________ Year ____________________ Pages ____________________

Memorable Quote	Page Number

Characters

Plot Summary

Notes

Rating ☆ ☆ ☆ ☆ ☆

Book Title ______

Author ______ Nationality ______

Genre ______ Year ______ Pages ______

Memorable Quote	Page Number

Characters

Plot Summary

Notes

Rating ☆ ☆ ☆ ☆ ☆

Book Title ______________________

Author ______________________ Nationality ______________________

Genre ______________________ Year ______________________ Pages ______________________

Memorable Quote	Page Number

Characters

Plot Summary

Notes

Rating ☆ ☆ ☆ ☆ ☆

Book Title ____________________

Author ____________ Nationality ____________

Genre ____________ Year ____________ Pages ________

Memorable Quote	Page Number

Characters

Plot Summary

Notes

Rating ☆ ☆ ☆ ☆ ☆

Book Title ____________________

Author ____________________ Nationality ____________________

Genre ____________________ Year ____________________ Pages ____________________

Memorable Quote	Page Number

Characters

Plot Summary

Notes

Rating ☆ ☆ ☆ ☆ ☆

Book Title ____________________

Author ____________________ Nationality ____________________

Genre ____________________ Year ____________________ Pages ____________________

Memorable Quote	Page Number

Characters

Plot Summary

Notes

Rating ☆ ☆ ☆ ☆ ☆

Book Title ______________________

Author ______________________ Nationality ______________________

Genre ______________________ Year ______________________ Pages ______________

Memorable Quote	Page Number

Characters

Plot Summary

Notes

Rating ☆ ☆ ☆ ☆ ☆

Book Title ______________________

Author ______________________ Nationality ______________________

Genre ______________________ Year ______________________ Pages ______________________

Memorable Quote	Page Number

Characters

Plot Summary

Notes

Rating ☆ ☆ ☆ ☆ ☆

Book Title ______________________

Author ______________________ Nationality ______________________

Genre ______________________ Year ______________________ Pages ______________________

Memorable Quote	Page Number

Characters

Plot Summary

Notes

Rating ☆ ☆ ☆ ☆ ☆

Book Title ______________________

Author ______________________ Nationality ______________________

Genre ______________________ Year ______________________ Pages ____________

Memorable Quote	Page Number

Characters

Plot Summary

Notes

Rating ☆ ☆ ☆ ☆ ☆

Book Title

Author

Nationality

Genre

Year

Pages

Memorable Quote	Page Number

Characters

Plot Summary

Notes

Rating ☆ ☆ ☆ ☆ ☆

Book Title ______________________

Author ______________________ Nationality ______________________

Genre ______________________ Year ______________________ Pages ______________

Memorable Quote	Page Number

Characters

Plot Summary

Notes

Rating ☆ ☆ ☆ ☆ ☆

Book Title ____________________

Author ____________________ Nationality ____________________

Genre ____________________ Year ____________________ Pages ____________

Memorable Quote	Page Number

Characters

Plot Summary

Notes

Rating ☆ ☆ ☆ ☆ ☆

Book Title ____________________

Author ________________ Nationality ________________

Genre ________________ Year ________________ Pages ________

Memorable Quote	Page Number

Characters

Plot Summary

Notes

Rating ☆ ☆ ☆ ☆ ☆

Book Title

Author

Nationality

Genre

Year

Pages

Memorable Quote	Page Number

Characters

Plot Summary

Notes

Rating ☆ ☆ ☆ ☆ ☆

Book Title ______________________

Author ______________ Nationality ______________

Genre ______________ Year ______________ Pages ________

Memorable Quote	Page Number

Characters

Plot Summary

Notes

Rating ☆ ☆ ☆ ☆ ☆

Book Title ______________________

Author ______________ Nationality ______________

Genre ______________ Year ______________ Pages ______________

Memorable Quote	Page Number

Characters

Plot Summary

Notes

Rating ☆ ☆ ☆ ☆ ☆

Book Title ______________________________

Author ____________________ Nationality ____________________

Genre ____________________ Year ____________________ Pages ____________

Memorable Quote	Page Number

Characters

Plot Summary

Notes

Rating ☆ ☆ ☆ ☆ ☆

Book Title ______________________

Author ______________________ Nationality ______________________

Genre ______________________ Year ______________________ Pages ______________________

Memorable Quote	Page Number

Characters

Plot Summary

Notes

Rating ☆ ☆ ☆ ☆ ☆

Book Title ______________________

Author ______________________ Nationality ______________________

Genre ______________________ Year ______________________ Pages ______________________

Memorable Quote	Page Number

Characters

Plot Summary

Notes

Rating ☆ ☆ ☆ ☆ ☆

Book Title ______________________

Author ______________________ Nationality ______________________

Genre ______________________ Year ______________________ Pages ______________________

Memorable Quote	Page Number

Characters

Plot Summary

Notes

Rating ☆ ☆ ☆ ☆ ☆

Book Title ______________________________

Author ____________________ Nationality ____________________

Genre ____________________ Year ____________________ Pages __________

Memorable Quote	Page Number

Characters

Plot Summary

Notes

Rating ☆ ☆ ☆ ☆ ☆

Book Title ______________________

Author ______________________ Nationality ______________________

Genre ______________________ Year ______________________ Pages ______________

Memorable Quote	Page Number

Characters

Plot Summary

Notes

Rating ☆ ☆ ☆ ☆ ☆

Book Title ______________________

Author ______________________ Nationality ______________

Genre ______________________ Year ______________ Pages ________

Memorable Quote	Page Number

Characters

Plot Summary

Notes

Rating ☆ ☆ ☆ ☆ ☆

Book Title ______________________

Author ______________________ Nationality ______________________

Genre ______________________ Year ______________________ Pages ____________

Memorable Quote	Page Number

Characters

Plot Summary

Notes

Rating ☆ ☆ ☆ ☆ ☆

Book Title ______________________

Author ______________________ Nationality ______________________

Genre ______________________ Year ______________________ Pages ______________

Memorable Quote	Page Number

Characters

Plot Summary

Notes

Rating ☆ ☆ ☆ ☆ ☆

Book Title ______________________

Author ______________________ Nationality ______________________

Genre ______________________ Year ______________________ Pages ______________

Memorable Quote	Page Number

Characters

Plot Summary

Notes

Rating ☆ ☆ ☆ ☆ ☆

Book Title ______________________

Author ______________________ Nationality ______________________

Genre ______________________ Year ______________________ Pages ____________

Memorable Quote	Page Number

Characters

Plot Summary

Notes

Rating ☆ ☆ ☆ ☆ ☆

Book Title ______________________

Author ______________________ Nationality ______________________

Genre ______________________ Year ______________________ Pages ______________________

Memorable Quote	Page Number

Characters

Plot Summary

Notes

Rating ☆ ☆ ☆ ☆ ☆

Book Title ______________________

Author ______________________ Nationality ______________________

Genre ______________________ Year ______________________ Pages ____________

Memorable Quote	Page Number

Characters

Plot Summary

Notes

Rating ☆ ☆ ☆ ☆ ☆

Book Title ____________________

Author ____________________ Nationality ____________________

Genre ____________________ Year ____________________ Pages ____________________

Memorable Quote	Page Number

Characters

Plot Summary

Notes

Rating ☆ ☆ ☆ ☆ ☆

Book Title ______________________

Author ______________________ Nationality ______________________

Genre ______________________ Year ______________________ Pages ______________________

Memorable Quote	Page Number

Characters

Plot Summary

Notes

Rating ☆ ☆ ☆ ☆ ☆

Book Title ____________________

Author ____________________ Nationality ____________________

Genre ____________________ Year ____________________ Pages ____________________

Memorable Quote	Page Number

Characters

Plot Summary

Notes

Rating ☆ ☆ ☆ ☆ ☆

Book Title ______________________

Author ______________ Nationality ______________

Genre ______________ Year ______________ Pages ________

Memorable Quote	Page Number

Characters

Plot Summary

Notes

Rating ☆ ☆ ☆ ☆ ☆

Book Title ______________________________

Author ______________________ Nationality ______________________

Genre ______________________ Year ______________________ Pages ____________

Memorable Quote	Page Number

Characters

Plot Summary

Notes

Rating ☆ ☆ ☆ ☆ ☆

Book Title ______________________________

Author ______________________ Nationality ______________

Genre ______________________ Year ______________ Pages ________

Memorable Quote	Page Number

Characters

Plot Summary

Notes

Rating ☆ ☆ ☆ ☆ ☆

Book Title ______________________

Author ______________________ Nationality ______________________

Genre ______________________ Year ______________________ Pages ____________

Memorable Quote	Page Number

Characters

Plot Summary

Notes

Rating ☆ ☆ ☆ ☆ ☆

Book Title ______________________

Author ______________________ Nationality ______________________

Genre ______________________ Year ______________________ Pages __________

Memorable Quote	Page Number

Characters

Plot Summary

Notes

Rating ☆ ☆ ☆ ☆ ☆

Book Title ______________________

Author ______________________ Nationality ______________________

Genre ______________________ Year ______________________ Pages ____________

Memorable Quote	Page Number

Characters

Plot Summary

Notes

Rating ☆ ☆ ☆ ☆ ☆

Book Title ______________________

Author ______________________ Nationality ______________________

Genre ______________________ Year ______________________ Pages ____________

Memorable Quote	Page Number

Characters

Plot Summary

Notes

Rating ☆ ☆ ☆ ☆ ☆

Book Title ______________________

Author ______________ Nationality ______________

Genre ______________ Year ______________ Pages ______________

Memorable Quote	Page Number

Characters

Plot Summary

Notes

Rating ☆ ☆ ☆ ☆ ☆

Book Title ______________________

Author ______________ Nationality ______________

Genre ______________ Year ______________ Pages ________

Memorable Quote	Page Number

Characters

Plot Summary

Notes

Rating ☆ ☆ ☆ ☆ ☆

Book Title ______________________

Author ______________________ Nationality ______________________

Genre ______________________ Year ______________________ Pages ______________________

Memorable Quote	Page Number

Characters

Plot Summary

Notes

Rating ☆ ☆ ☆ ☆ ☆

Book Title ______________________

Author ______________________ Nationality ______________________

Genre ______________________ Year ______________________ Pages ____________

Memorable Quote	Page Number

Characters

Plot Summary

Notes

Rating ☆ ☆ ☆ ☆ ☆

Book Title ______________________

Author ______________________ Nationality ______________________

Genre ______________________ Year ______________________ Pages ______________________

Memorable Quote	Page Number

Characters

Plot Summary

Notes

Rating ☆ ☆ ☆ ☆ ☆

Book Title ______________________

Author ______________ Nationality ______________

Genre ______________ Year ______________ Pages ________

Memorable Quote	Page Number

Characters

Plot Summary

Notes

Rating ☆ ☆ ☆ ☆ ☆

Book Title

Author

Nationality

Genre

Year

Pages

Memorable Quote	Page Number

Characters

Plot Summary

Notes

Rating ☆ ☆ ☆ ☆ ☆

Book Title ______________________

Author ______________________ Nationality ______________________

Genre ______________________ Year ______________________ Pages ______________

Memorable Quote	Page Number

Characters

Plot Summary

Notes

Rating ☆ ☆ ☆ ☆ ☆

Book Title ______________________

Author ______________ Nationality ______________

Genre ______________ Year ______________ Pages ________

Memorable Quote	Page Number

Characters

Plot Summary

Notes

Rating ☆ ☆ ☆ ☆ ☆

Book Title ____________________

Author ____________ Nationality ____________

Genre ____________ Year ____________ Pages ________

Memorable Quote	Page Number

Characters

Plot Summary

Notes

Rating ☆ ☆ ☆ ☆ ☆

Book Title

Author

Nationality

Genre

Year

Pages

Memorable Quote	Page Number

Characters

Plot Summary

Notes

Rating ☆ ☆ ☆ ☆ ☆

Book Title ______________________

Author ______________________ Nationality ______________________

Genre ______________________ Year ______________________ Pages ____________

Memorable Quote	Page Number

Characters

Plot Summary

Notes

Rating ☆ ☆ ☆ ☆ ☆

Book Title ______________________________

Author ______________________ Nationality ______________

Genre ______________________ Year ______________ Pages ________

Memorable Quote	Page Number

Characters

Plot Summary

Notes

Rating ☆ ☆ ☆ ☆ ☆

Book Title ______________________

Author ______________________ Nationality ______________________

Genre ______________________ Year ______________________ Pages ______________________

Memorable Quote	Page Number

Characters

Plot Summary

Notes

Rating ☆ ☆ ☆ ☆ ☆

Book Title ____________________

Author ____________________ Nationality ____________________

Genre ____________________ Year ____________________ Pages __________

Memorable Quote	Page Number

Characters

Plot Summary

Notes

Rating ☆ ☆ ☆ ☆ ☆

Book Title ______________________

Author ______________________ Nationality ______________________

Genre ______________________ Year ______________________ Pages ____________

Memorable Quote	Page Number

Characters

Plot Summary

Notes

Rating ☆ ☆ ☆ ☆ ☆

Book Title ____________________

Author ____________________ Nationality ____________________

Genre ____________________ Year ____________________ Pages ____________

Memorable Quote	Page Number

Characters

Plot Summary

Notes

Rating ☆ ☆ ☆ ☆ ☆

Book Title ______________________________

Author ______________________ Nationality ______________________

Genre ______________________ Year ______________________ Pages ____________

Memorable Quote	Page Number

Characters

Plot Summary

Notes

Rating ☆ ☆ ☆ ☆ ☆

Book Title

Author Nationality

Genre Year Pages

Memorable Quote	Page Number

Characters

Plot Summary

Notes

Rating ☆ ☆ ☆ ☆ ☆

Book Title ______________________

Author ______________ Nationality ______________

Genre ______________ Year ______________ Pages ______

Memorable Quote	Page Number

Characters

Plot Summary

Notes

Rating ☆ ☆ ☆ ☆ ☆

Book Title ______________________

Author ______________ Nationality ______________

Genre ______________ Year ______________ Pages ________

Memorable Quote	Page Number

Characters

Plot Summary

Notes

Rating ☆ ☆ ☆ ☆ ☆

Book Title ______________________

Author ______________ Nationality ______________

Genre ______________ Year ______________ Pages ________

Memorable Quote	Page Number

Characters

Plot Summary

Notes

Rating ☆ ☆ ☆ ☆ ☆

Book Title ______________________

Author ______________________ Nationality ______________________

Genre ______________________ Year ______________________ Pages ____________

Memorable Quote	Page Number

Characters

Plot Summary

Notes

Rating ☆ ☆ ☆ ☆ ☆

Book Title ______________________

Author ______________________ Nationality ______________________

Genre ______________________ Year ______________________ Pages ______________________

Memorable Quote	Page Number

Characters

Plot Summary

Notes

Rating ☆ ☆ ☆ ☆ ☆

Book Title ______________________

Author ______________________ Nationality ______________________

Genre ______________________ Year ______________________ Pages ____________

Memorable Quote	Page Number

Characters

Plot Summary

Notes

Rating ☆ ☆ ☆ ☆ ☆

Book Title ______________________

Author ______________________ Nationality ______________________

Genre ______________________ Year ______________________ Pages ______________

Memorable Quote	Page Number

Characters

Plot Summary

Notes

Rating ☆ ☆ ☆ ☆ ☆

Book Title ______________________

Author ______________________ Nationality ______________________

Genre ______________________ Year ______________________ Pages ______________________

Memorable Quote	Page Number

Characters

Plot Summary

Notes

Rating ☆ ☆ ☆ ☆ ☆

My Wishlist And Notes

73256788R00068

Made in the
USA
Middletown, DE